# I Keep Working!

Getting It Done!

Leona Fowler



SOCIAL AND EMOTIONAL LEARNING FOR THE REAL WORLD™

Rosen Classroom™

There are many things to do today.

Keep working.
You can get it done!

Kara folds clothes.
She gets the job done.

Adam rakes the yard.
It takes a long time!

Tia makes cookies.
She makes a lot!

Alice writes a story.
She works hard.

Eric helps out.
He takes out the trash.

Lily has a dog.
She feeds the dog.

Sam puts away the dishes.
He is careful.

What do you have to do today?
You can do it!

# Words to Know

clothes

cookies

dishes

trash